CHAIR CANING
& SEAT WEAVING
HANDBOOK

By Editors of Skills Institute Press

Illustrated Directions for Cane, Rush, and Tape Seats

skills institute press

Distributed By
Fox Chapel Publishing

Fox Chapel
PUBLISHING

Chair Caning & Seat Weaving Handbook is an original work, first published in 2012.

Portions of text and art previously published by and reproduced under license with Direct Holdings Americas Inc.

Special thanks to Shaker Workshops for providing the photos on page 7 and the photos indicated on pages 24 and 25. To learn more, please visit *www.shakerworkshops.com*.

Special thanks to Planet Art/Chair Repair for providing the photos indicated on pages 24 and 25. Photos by Tipton Gentry of Portable Onsite Photography. To learn more, please visit *http://gochairrepair.com*.

Special thanks to Brandy Clements, Dave Klingler, and Tara Fitzkee for their generous assistance in providing technical advice for this title.

ISBN 978-1-56523-556-4

Library of Congress Cataloging-in-Publication Data

Chair Caning & Seat Weaving Handbook.
        pages cm
 Summary: "This book will detail the basics of making chair seats, from weaving with cloth tape, rush, or cane to simple upholstery with cloth or leather. Also covers chair repair"-- Provided by publisher.
    ISBN 978-1-56523-556-4 (pbk.)
    1. Furniture making. 2. Chair caning. 3. Rush-work. 4. Furniture making. I. Skills Institute Press. II. Title: Chair Caning and Seat Weaving Handbook.
    TT199.C36 2012
    684.08--dc23
                            2011053239

To learn more about the other great books from Fox Chapel Publishing,
or to find a retailer near you, call toll-free 800-457-9112 or visit us at
www.FoxChapelPublishing.com.

We are always looking for talented authors. To submit an idea, please send a brief inquiry to
acquisitions@foxchapelpublishing.com.

Printed in China
Third printing

Contents

Seats

The seat is the reason for a chair's existence. Backs and arms may be optional—even legs—but every chair needs a seat. Over the centuries, chair makers have settled on many seat styles to suit a variety of applications and uses. In this book, you will find techniques for making three types of seats: a woven cane seat, a rush seat, and a tape seat.

The practice of weaving chair seats has a long history. Western chair makers have used cane to make seats for chairs and stools since the sixteenth century, while the Egyptians were making rush seats more than 3,000 years ago. Although caning a seat requires few tools *(page 5)*, it is a time-consuming process that demands patience and practice. Using a caning kit for practice is an excellent option. Weaving a typical cane seat will take at least 12 hours. A less time-consuming option is prewoven caning, which is wedged into a groove around the seat frame, as shown on page 17. Prewoven cane can only be used if your seat contains a pre-cut groove, or if you cut a groove to house the cane into the chair seat.

Today, rush seats are generally woven with twisted kraft paper rather than natural rush—except on reproduction pieces. Sold in various widths and colors, fiber rush seats are very durable. Rushing a seat, as shown on page 26, is an easier technique to master than caning, and is an excellent way to span the seat frame of a stick chair.

Tape became popular as a woven seat material after 1830. A woven, cotton material, tape does not wear as quickly as materials like cane and rush. Because tape seats are usually made following a simple woven pattern, they can be produced much faster than cane or rush seats, which involve more complex processes and patterns.

Although woven seats are intended to last a long time, they usually do not last as long as the chair itself. The chair being rewoven on page 18, for example, is more than a hundred years old. Before reweaving an old cane seat, be sure to remove any fasteners from the edges of the seat frame.

SEAT STYLES

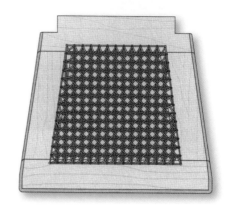

Cane seat *(page 8)*
Seat consists of a frame joined by mortise-and-tenon or plate joints. Cane is hand-woven in individual strands; prewoven cane can also be glued into a groove routed around the seat. Seat is usually fastened to the seat rails.

Rush seat *(page 26)*
Strands of fiber or kraft paper are woven across the posts and rails of a stick chair; provides a sturdy seat that is simple and inexpensive to apply and renew.

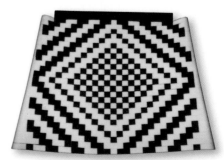

Shaker tape seat *(page 18)*
Shaker tape is a sturdy material that can be used on a variety of chair frames to create a lasting, colorful seat. Shaker tape can be woven into a wide array of patterns.

THE BASIC SUPPLIES

CANE

You will typically purchase cane in bundles called hanks, made of 10- to 20-foot lengths, totaling 1,000 feet. This amount of cane is usually enough to make two to three chair seats. The chart below shows the various widths of cane available and the diameter of the holes you need to *drill* through the frame to accept the strands. For each chair, you will need weaving cane and binding cane.

SCISSORS/SHEARS

A sharp knife is needed to cut the cane, producing a clean edge that is less likely to fray than a ragged edge. You can also use a good pair of shears or heavy-duty scissors, as long as the final result is a nice, clean edge to the cane.

PEGS

Wooden pegs are used to hold the strands of cane in the holes of the seat frame as you work. These can be purchased from a specialty supplier or fashioned out of wooden dowels. You can even choose to use golf tees. At the end of the caning process, a peg will be *hammered* into each of the four corner holes of the seat and secured with *wood glue*.

BUCKET

To effectively make a cane chair seat, the cane must be kept soft and flexible. Fill a bucket with warm water and keep strands of cane in it while you work. When you remove a strand of cane from the water, remember to replace it with a new one. Some furniture makers like to add *glycerine* to the water to make the cane even easier to thread.

AWL

An awl is a good tool to have on hand when caning, as it allows you to easily separate strands of cane when needed during the weaving process.

WOODEN WEDGES

Wooden wedges are used to fit prewoven cane into a groove cut in a chair seat's frame. Once the cane has been fit, a *chisel* and *wooden mallet* are used to trim the excess, and *reed splines* are glued and hammered into place to hold the cane.

The most basic caning supplies include cane, wooden pegs, a hammer, and a knife. Other tools and supplies that you might want to have on hand are wood glue, a bucket, an awl, and glycerine.

Cane Size	Actual Width	Metric Width	Hole Diameter	Holes Center to Center
Super Fine		2 mm	1/8"	3/8"
Fine Fine		2.25 mm	3/16"	1/2"
Fine		2.5 mm	3/16"	5/8"
Narrow Medium		2.75 mm	1/4"	3/4"
Medium		3 mm	1/4"	3/4"
Common		3.5 mm	5/16"	7/8"

TAPE

Shaker *tape*, also known as listing, is an incredibly durable material perfect for making long-lasting chair seats. It comes in a variety of colors and even patterns, allowing furniture makers to produce a variety of designs. The tape weaving process is very simple. Tape is secured to the side rail of a chair using *tacks* and a *hammer*. The warp rows are woven and are stuffed with *foam padding* cut to size using a *craft knife*. Sewing supplies like a needle and thread are good to have on hand to piece lengths of tape together. Overlapping the end of two pieces of tape in the weaving is another way to accomplish this.

TAPING SUPPLIES

Creating a chair seat using tape is a very simple process and requires these tools:

- Shaker tape
- Tacks
- Hammer
- 1"-thick foam padding
- Craft knife
- Needle and thread (optional)
- Scissors/shears
- Spring clamps
- Awl

RUSHING SUPPLIES

Rush in furniture making originally referred to cattail leaves twisted together to form long strands. Today, rush is made up of fiber paper, twisted together in a manner similar to that used for the cattail leaves. During the seat-making process, rush is attached to the side rail of the chair using *tacks* and a *hammer*. It is then looped around the rungs of the chair following a distinctive pattern. Halfway through the wrapping process, the rush is stuffed with *cardboard* to provide extra padding.

RUSHING SUPPLIES

Creating a rush seat requires only a few basic supplies:

- Rush
- Tacks
- Hammer
- Cardboard
- Awl
- Spring clamps
- Flathead screwdriver

Woven Seat Patterns

This book teaches you how to create a basic cane seat and shaker tape seat. This does not mean you are limited to making seats using only those patterns, however. The beauty of cane and shaker tape is that they can be woven in many different ways to create many different patterns. The following are some patterns to inspire you. You can try to recreate one of these patterns or develop one of your own.

CANING PATTERNS

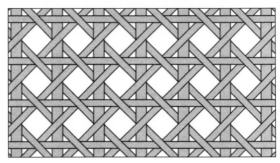

Five-way standard

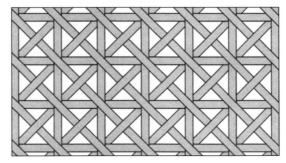

Single Victoria

Star

Lace

TAPING PATTERNS

Shaker tape comes in a wide array of colors and can be used to create a variety of woven patterns. The diamond patterns featured on these chairs were all made using shaker tape. See if you can develop your own unique woven diamond pattern, or use one of these patterns as inspiration when creating your own shaker tape seat. Use graph paper to sketch your pattern and then follow your design to weave the seat. Photos courtesy of Shaker Workshops, *www.shakerworkshops.com*.

CHAPTER 1

Cane Seats

This chapter will show you how to cane a chair seat by hand. Although the process is laborious—it takes at least 12 hours to weave a seat for a typical chair— the result is both sturdy and elegant. As shown on the following pages, the first step involves making a frame and fastening it to the seat rails. The cane is anchored to this frame.

As mentioned previously, cane is usually sold in bundles called hanks. The chart on page 5 shows the various widths of cane available and the diameter of the holes you need to drill through the frame to accept the strands. The only other special supplies required are wooden pegs to hold the strands of cane in the holes as you weave them, but golf tees will do.

There are a few rules you should follow as you cane a seat. To keep the strands flexible, keep two or three in a bucket of warm water for 15 to 20 minutes, replacing each one as it is used. Don't soak the cane too long or it will turn gray. Some people add glycerine to make the cane easier to thread. Should a length dry and become brittle as you weave it, you can sponge a bit of water onto it. Always keep the cane's glossy side up. Do not allow the cane to twist, especially under the seat frame or in the holes. Also, the cane can only be woven in one direction; otherwise, it will catch and break. Run a fingernail along the glossy side and you will notice a bump every foot or so. Each bump is a leaf node. Your nail will catch on the nodes in one direction, but not in the other. Weave the cane in the direction that allows you to pull the leaf nodes through the holes without catching. When a length of cane comes to an end, peg it in a hole, trim it to leave an excess of about 5 inches, and start a new length up through the adjacent hole.

Chair caning traces its origins to medieval China. It was introduced in America in the second half of the seventeenth century and has experienced a revival since the 1940s. The process is time-consuming but not difficult to master. The result is a chair seat that can last decades. This chair seat is almost complete; wooden pegs still need to be added to the corners.

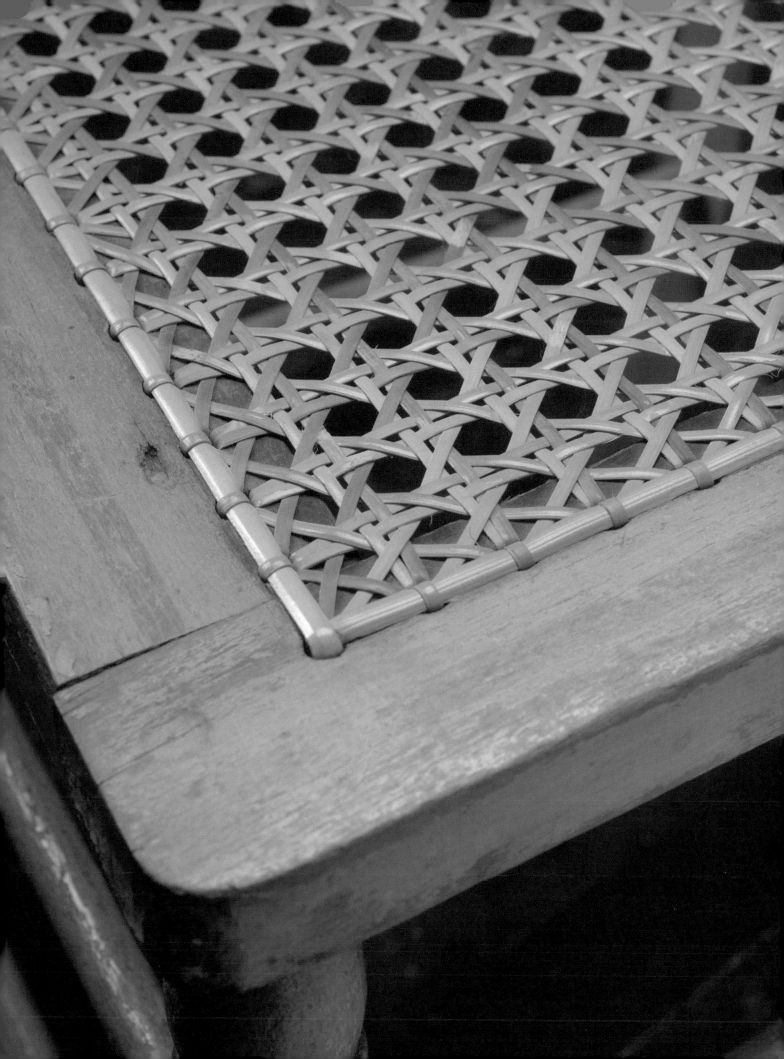

MAKING THE CANING FRAME

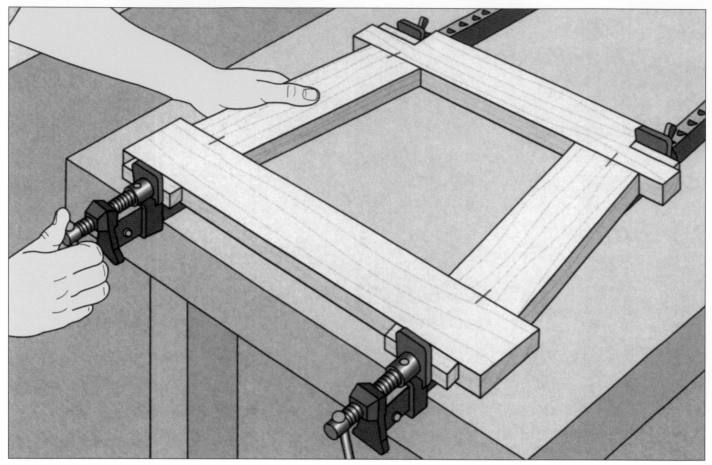

Making the frame

The simplest way to repair a cane seat is to remove the old cane and weave a new seat using the old seat frame. If the seat frame is also in need of repair, you can build a new one and weave a new cane seat. If you wish to make a new frame for your chair, use the old seat to determine the dimensions of the caning frame. Each of the four pieces should be about 3½ inches wide and can overhang the front and side rails of the seat rails by approximately ½ inch, if you wish. Cut notches for the rear legs in the back frame piece, then glue the pieces together, using a mortise-and-tenon or biscuit joint at each corner. When clamping, protect your stock with wood pads *(above)*.

Preparing the frame for caning

Once the glue has cured, cut the frame to final size, then mark a line all around the frame ½ inch from the inside edges. Add a mark along the line in the middle of the front and back rails. Then refer to the chart on page 5 to find the spacing and diameter of the holes required for the width of cane you are using. Mark the holes along the line, adjusting the spacing, if necessary, to ensure that the holes will be equidistant. Then install a brad-point bit of the correct diameter in your drill press. Set the frame on the table, align a corner mark under the bit, and clamp a board to the table flush against the edge of the frame as a guide. Bore a hole through the frame at each mark, holding the stock against the edge guide *(right)*. Once all the holes are drilled, twist a piece of sandpaper into a cone and smooth the holes so that there will be no sharp edges that might tear the cane.

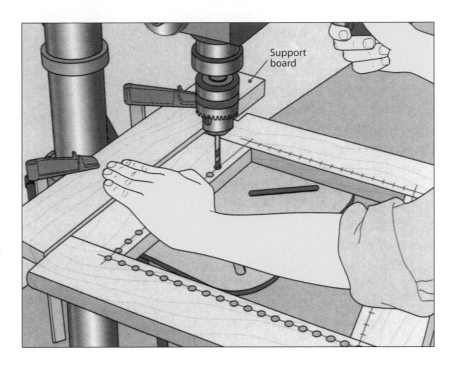

WEAVING THE CANE

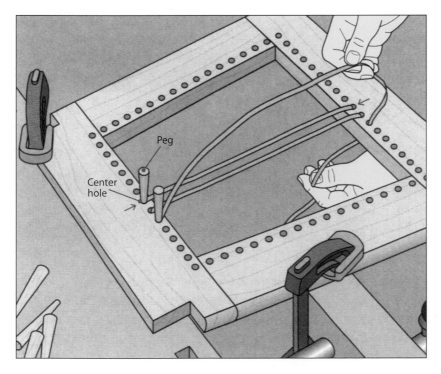

Weaving the first vertical rows

If you are weaving cane into a new seat frame, clamp the frame to a workbench so the holes are unobstructed, and use sandpaper to round the inside edge of the frame. If you are replacing the cane in an existing chair, sand the inside edge of the seat frame as described previously, and place the chair between your legs, holding it firmly with your thighs. Then take a length of cane from your bucket and feed it from above into the center hole in the back frame piece. Leave about 5 inches hanging below the frame and insert a peg into the hole to secure the strand. Now bring the strand across the frame and through the top of the center hole in the front piece; pull it taut and peg it. The cane should be taut enough that if you pluck it, it will make a sound similar to a guitar string. Pass the strand up through the adjacent hole on the front piece and bring it across to the back piece, feeding it down from the top into the hole next to where you started. Continue in this fashion *(left)*, moving one hole sideways and up and then across the frame, always transferring the peg from the last hole. Leave the first peg in place as well as any peg securing the end or start of a strand. Keep the washcloth in your bucket and use it to wet the strand of cane as needed as you work. Note: Every chair is different, and the chair you're working on might have two center holes, no center hole, or a center hole only in the front or back of the frame. If this is the case, line up the cane visually between holes to create straight rows.

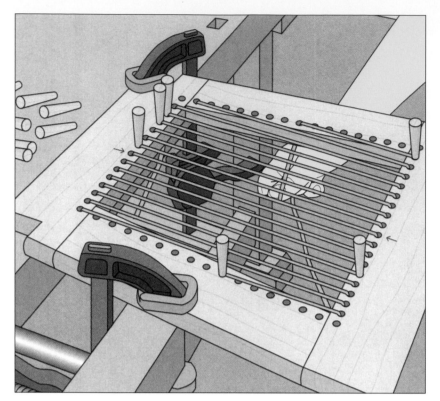

Keeping the rows parallel

If your caning frame is trapezoidal rather than square, as in the example shown here, you will have to peg the strands in a hole in the side piece, rather than the front or back, as you reach the side of the frame. This will keep the last row parallel to the preceding ones. When you get to the side piece, choose the appropriate hole and feed the caning into it as described in the previous step. Once this is done, return to the hole adjacent to where you started and weave the cane toward the opposite side. Remember to peg the cane at the beginning and end of each strand, leaving about 5 inches hanging below the frame.

Installing the first horizontal rows

Once the first set of vertical rows has been installed, move on to the first horizontal row. Start with the first hole in one side piece at the back of the frame. Remove the peg from the hole if there is one, then feed the cane up through the hole and insert a peg to secure the strand. Pull the strand over the frame and the vertical rows already in place, and secure the cane into the first hole in the opposite side piece, using a peg. Continue to weave horizontal rows as you did the vertical rows, working from the back toward the front of the frame.

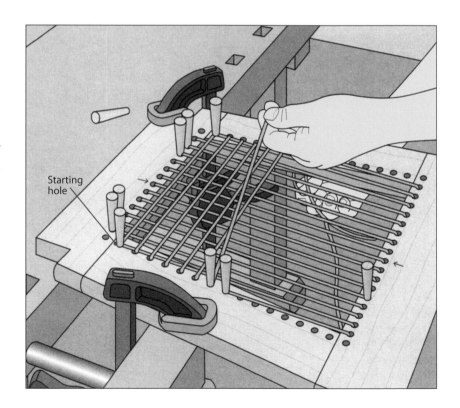

Starting hole

Adding the second vertical rows

Weave the second vertical row as you did the first, passing the cane over all the strands in place. However, instead of starting at the middle of the back rail, begin with the last hole you pegged in the first vertical row in the left side of the seat frame. Then, weave the cane from this point *(right)* toward the opposite side, aligning the strands slightly to the right or the left of the first set of vertical strands. Note: You can align the cane in the second vertical row to the right or the left of the first row, as long as the alignment is consistently to one side or the other.

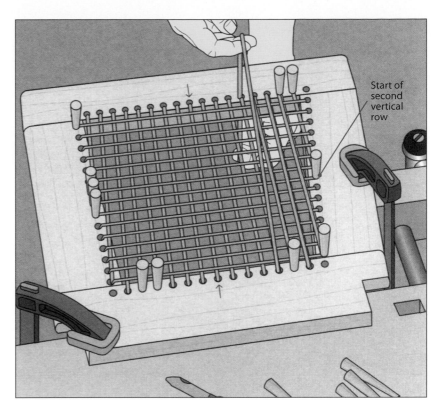

Start of second vertical row

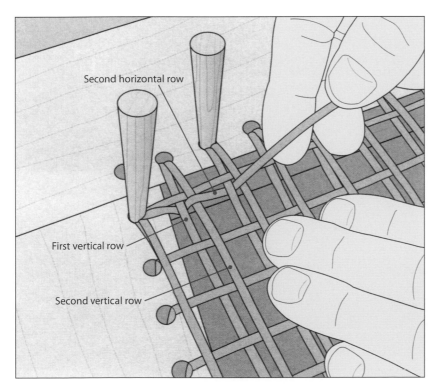

Second horizontal row

First vertical row

Second vertical row

Weaving the second horizontal rows

Before starting this step, turn your chair upside down and place a damp towel over the back of the cane, leaving it on the cane for about ten minutes. Then, turn your chair upright and wet a strand of cane to weave the second horizontal rows. Start with the same hole in which you started the first horizontal row and peg the strand in place. Then, weave the cane under the first vertical row and over the second one, positioning the cane beside the first horizontal row *(left)*. Continue weaving in this way until you reach the seat front, and peg the last strand in place. Note: Watch the cane as you work. If it seems to be bending out of shape, you may need to weave it over the first vertical row and under the second one and repeat. Once you have finished weaving the second horizontal rows, use your fingers to push the cane into a grid pattern. You might be tempted to do this earlier as you are weaving, but it is best to wait until all the vertical and horizontal rows are complete. Once you have completed this step, secure as many of the loose strands of cane as possible by turning the chair over, wetting the loose strands of cane and the loops of cane on the bottom of the chair, and tying the strands in place (see page 15).

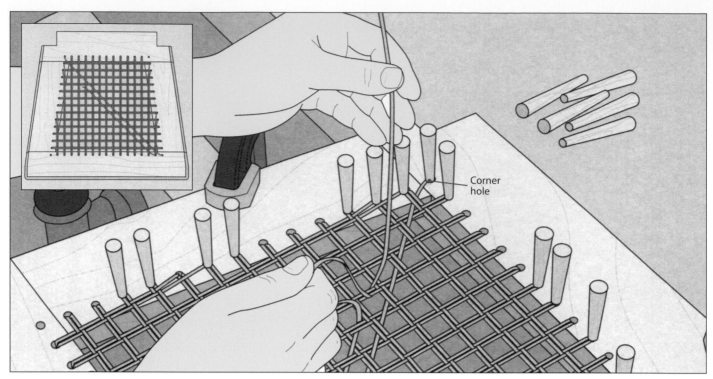

Corner hole

Weaving the first diagonal rows

For this step, you want the cane to be slightly dry, so only soak it for about a minute. Then, peg the cane in one of the left-hand corner holes at the *back* of the frame. Wet the tip of the cane and pass it over the horizontal strands and under the vertical strands to the immediate right, tucking the cane into the corners of the grid pattern formed by the horizontal and vertical rows. It is very important that you keep the tip of the cane wet as you work. If you see the cane bending out of shape, try weaving it over the vertical strands and under the horizontal strands. Continue until you reach the opposite corner hole. Then pass the strand up through the hole

in the front frame piece next to the corner hole and work your way toward the back of the seat, weaving the cane under the vertical rows and over the horizontal ones. Continue weaving diagonal rows this way until you reach the other corner hole in the front of the seat, making sure that all the rows are parallel. It is helpful if you weave the tip of the cane over and under several of the vertical/horizontal rows, and then pull the rest of the strand through, using your fingers to make sure the cane does not twist as you pull it. Now, move to the hole in the back of the chair frame next to where you started the diagonal rows and repeat the process, working in the opposite direction.

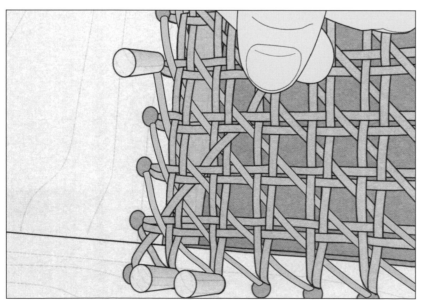

Weaving the second diagonal rows

Start the second diagonal weave in the left-hand corner hole in the *front* of the chair frame. This time, feed the cane over the vertical rows and under the horizontal ones *(left)*, or under the vertical rows and over the horizontal rows if you wove your first diagonal row over the vertical rows and under the horizontal rows. Complete the rows as before. Use tweezers to remove any hairs that bunch up along the strands of cane as you work.

Tying off the loose ends of cane

Once the second diagonal row is done, secure any remaining loose strands hanging under the frame. Turn the seat frame over, wet the strands of cane and the loops of cane along the frame bottom, and use a double-loop knot *(inset)* or a half-hitch knot to secure each strand. To tie a double-loop knot, slip a loose strand under an adjacent strap of cane using an awl. Then feed it through the loop you just created *(right)*, pass it under the strap again and cinch it. Trim the remaining portion, leaving a ½-inch-long tip.

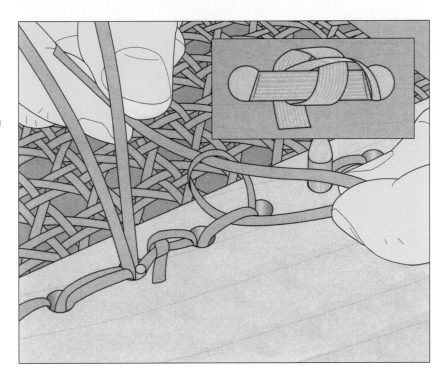

Applying the binder cane

Once the weaving is done and all the ends have been tied off, apply a strip of binder cane around the perimeter of the seat to give it a neat and finished appearance. Binder cane is usually one or two sizes larger than the cane used for the weave. Before adding the binder cane, examine the holes around the perimeter of the frame and make sure there is room to pass two more pieces of cane through them. Shift the previously woven pieces of cane with an awl to make room as needed. Note: The strands of cane that make up the diagonal rows should cross to form X's along the edges of the frame. Soak the binder cane and pass one end down through the left-back corner hole and peg it in place. Lay the binder cane across the row of holes in the back frame piece, then, select a length of weaving cane smaller than the one you used for the seat to anchor the binder cane. Soak the weaving cane, tie one end off underneath the frame, and tie loops over the binder cane by passing the weaving strand up through the first hole adjacent to the corner, over the binder cane, and back down through the same hole *(left)*. Move on to the next hole in the back of the seat frame and repeat, continuing until you reach the corner hole at the end of the piece. Trim off the excess length of binder cane at both ends and use new lengths along the remaining frame pieces.

Weaving cane

Binder cane

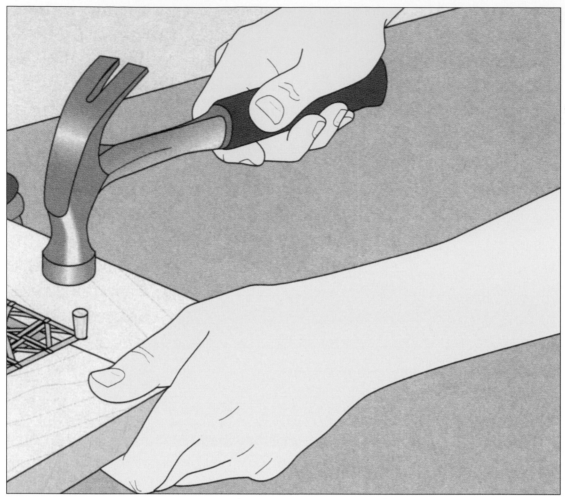

Pegging the corners

Once all the binder cane is installed, tie off the ends of the weaving cane you used to anchor it. At each corner, pull the binder cane taut and temporarily tap a peg into the corner hole. Mark the peg at the point where it meets the top of the frame piece, remove the peg and trim it at the mark. Spread a little glue on the sides of the peg and tap it in place with a hammer *(above)*. If necessary, trim the peg flush using a utility knife or small saw. Use scissors to trim away any hairs along the strands of cane. Cane has a natural coating that does not accept stain well. If you'd like to stain your cane seat, practice on some scrap pieces to ensure you get the look you want, or take your chair to a professional. To keep your cane seat from wearing, turn it over and cover the cane with a wet towel every three months if you keep the chair in or near direct sunlight. If you keep the chair inside away from sunlight, this can be done once or twice a year.

PREWOVEN CANE

Prewoven cane

Inspect your prewoven cane before use for any defects or problems due to age. Cut a piece of the cane so that it is 2 inches larger on all sides than the opening in your chair seat or back. Soak the cane in warm water in a flat bucket or bathtub for 30 minutes. The soaking will make the cane more pliable and easier to work. If desired, refinish your chair before installing the cane. Once the chair is ready, position the cane over the chair seat or back, making sure the rows of cane align with the edges of the frame. If caning the back of the chair, place the chair on its back for this process. Use a wedge to press the cane into the center of the groove in the back frame piece. Pull the cane taut across the opening and secure the cane in the center of the groove in the front of the frame. Repeat with the two side pieces. Then, begin adding wedges 2 inches to either side of the original wedges, starting in the back, moving to the front, and then to the two sides. It is important to secure each double row of cane in the groove with a wedge. Continue working around the frame in this manner, adding wedges at 2-inch intervals until all the cane is secured in place.

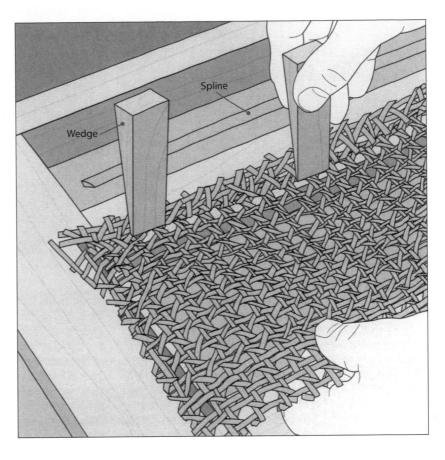

Securing the cane

Cut the reed splines that will hold the cane to fit in the grooves, mitering both ends of each piece, then work on one side of the frame at a time to fix the cane in place permanently. Starting with the front side of the frame, score the cane every few inches with a utility knife. Then, use a chisel and wooden mallet to trim the excess cane flush with the outside edge of the channel. Once the cane has been trimmed, remove the wedges, and put a line of glue in the channel. Pound the spline in place with the mallet. Wipe away any glue squeeze out, then repeat the process with the back of the frame *(left)* and the two sides. Note: If your chair has rounded corners, soak each spline before hammering it in place.

CHAPTER 2

Tape Seats

Shaker tape, called listing by the Shakers, began to supplant other types of woven seat materials after 1830. Its range of colors, neat appearance, durability, and ease of installation made it ideal for furniture builders bent on producing quality goods as efficiently as possible. And unlike cane or other naturally occurring materials, tape does not dry out or split; nor does it pinch or snag clothing.

Shown below and on the following pages, weaving is fairly simple. One length of tape, called the warp, is anchored to the side rails and wrapped around the front and back seat rails in adjoining rows. A second length, called the weft, is woven alternately under and over the strands that form the warp. Loose ends are joined by weaving them back on themselves or sewing them together, ensuring that the rows always remain parallel.

Shaker tape is available in ⅝- and 1-inch widths from folk-art suppliers. You can weave the basic tabby style shown in this section or create a wide variety of designs that include basic and complex geometric shapes.

The Shaker rocking chair shown above features canvas tape seating as well as a tape back.

WEAVING A TAPE SEAT

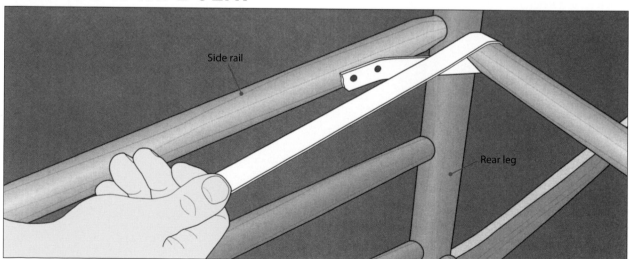

Side rail

Rear leg

Anchoring the warp rows

If your chair seat is square, tack a length of tape to the inside of a side seat rail about 2 inches from the rear leg so that the tape is parallel to the rail. Use an awl to create holes for the tacks, then hammer them in place. Note: Only use steel tacks. Loop the tape around the back rail from underneath, ensuring the edge of the material butts against the rear leg (above). Wrap the tape around the front rail and pull it toward the back rail from underneath. If your chair seat is not square, measure the difference in length between the longer and shorter rails and divide the result in half. Measure this amount along the front rail from each of the front legs and make a mark on the rail. Then, secure your tape to the side rail as described previously, loop it around the back rail, and wrap it around the front rail, aligning the edge of the tape with the mark on the front rail.

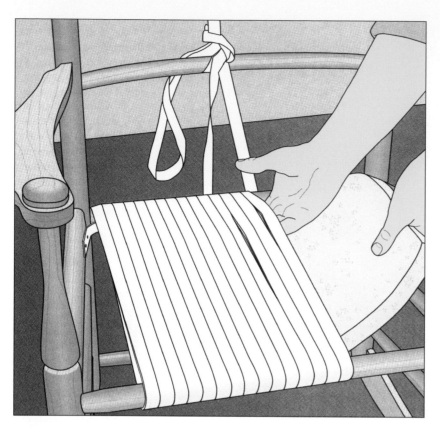

Stuffing the seat

Continue wrapping the warp around the front and back rails from underneath, making sure the adjoining rows of tape are in contact. The weave should be tight, but not so taut that there is no play for the weft rows to be woven between the warp rows. Once you are about halfway to the opposite side rail, it is time to stuff the seat. To prevent the tape from slackening, clamp the loose length of tape to the seat frame. If your chair is *very* sturdy, you can tie to loose end of tape to one of the back rails. Buy a piece of 1-inch-thick foam padding from a craft supply or hardware store and cut it with a craft knife to fit within the seat rails. Slip the padding between the tape layers *(left)*, centering it between the rails.

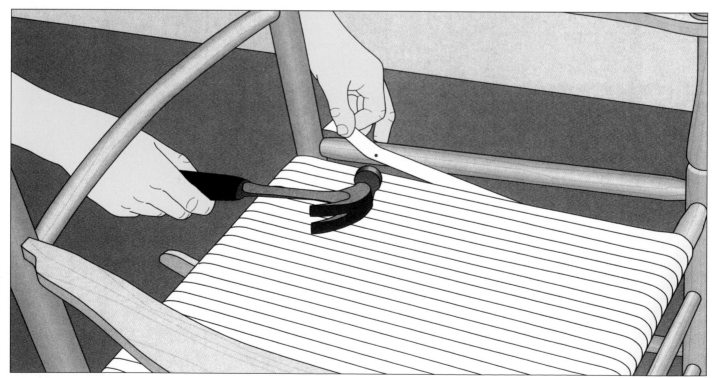

Completing the warp

Continue weaving the warp rows until you reach the opposite side rail and the back seat rail is entirely wrapped in tape. Then temporarily tack the loose length of tape to the side rail *(above)* and cut off the loose end, leaving a tail about 4 or 5 inches long.

Starting the weft

Set the chair upside down on a work surface that will enable you to work comfortably. Starting along the back seat rail opposite the place where you began the warp, slip the end of the weft tape under the first strand of the warp, over the next, and continue with this under-and-over weave until you reach the last warp strand. Pull the excess tape through, leaving 5 inches or so at the starting point. Tack this part to the side rail. Flip the chair upright and continue weaving on the top side of the seat.

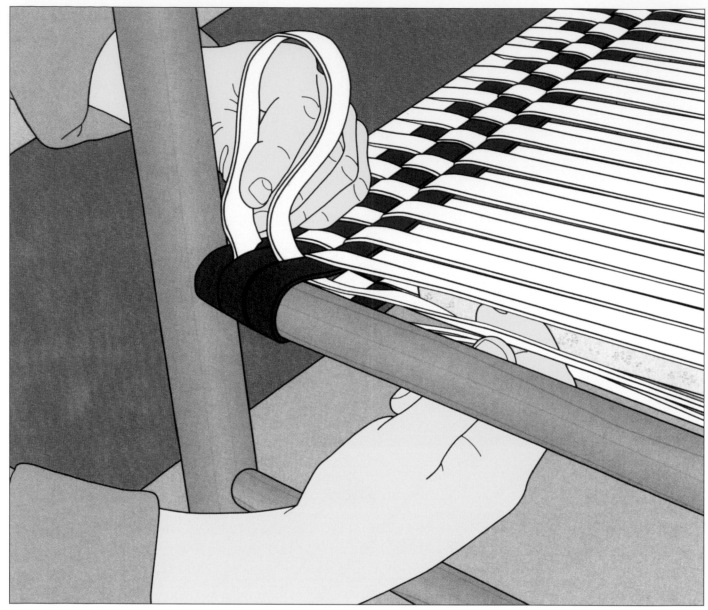

Filling the gaps in the warp

Weave about three rows of weft, then begin filling in the triangular gaps left along the side rails where you installed the warp. Cut a length of warp tape long enough to weave two rows of seating, plus about 5 inches, and slip the tape under the last strand of weft beneath the seat and around the front seat rail, butting it against the last row of warp you wove previously. Then return to the back rail, passing the tape under the last weft row and over the second one *(above)*. Weave another warp row adjacent to the last one the same way. Leave the excess hanging for now; you will be able to weave it into the subsequent weft rows. Weave three more weft rows and repeat the gap-filling process.

Completing the weft rows

Continue weaving the weft, wrapping each row around the side rails and weaving over and under the warp rows *(right)*. Avoid twisting the material. As you finish each row, pull it tight against the previous one with your fingers. As you work your way toward the side rail, the warp will become increasingly tight. To make space for the weft, slide a blunt knife between the warp rows as necessary. When you have laid down the final weft row, weave it back on itself to hold it in place. Also weave in any loose ends of tape on the underside of the seat.

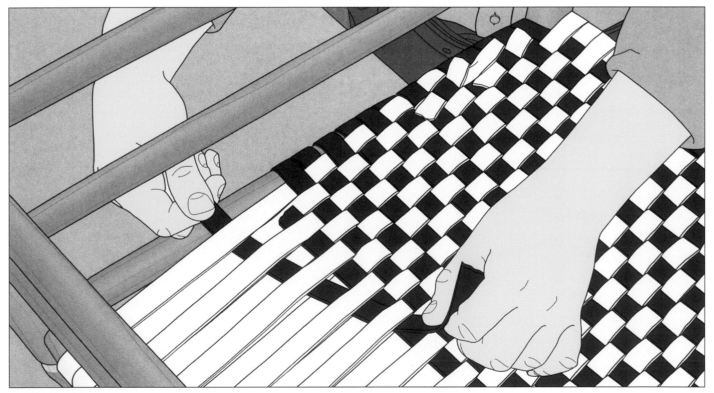

Splicing tape

If you run out of tape before finishing the warp or the weft, you will need to join two ends. You can start weaving a new length at a point about 6 inches before the end of the first tape *(above),* overlapping the tapes and binding them together by friction, but the pieces can separate over time.

A more effective method is to stitch the two pieces of tape together. Use this technique on the underside of the seat with the chair upside down so that no seams or bulges will be visible.

THE VERSATILITY OF SHAKER TAPE

Shaker tape can be used in a variety of patterns on a variety of chair frames to create a unique piece for your home. Presented here are some finished chairs to show you the vast options shaker tape provides. Use shaker tape to create a formal dining chair, or use it to spruce up your family's Kennedy rocker—the choices are endless.

Shaker back side chair with chevron seat and back pattern. Photo courtesy of Shaker Workshops, *www.shakerworkshops.com*.

Shaker straight chair with checkerboard seat pattern. Photo courtesy of Shaker Workshops, *www.shakerworkshops.com*.

Ebony Shaker back side chair with checkerboard seat and back pattern. Photo courtesy of Shaker Workshops, *www.shakerworkshops.com*.

Shaker back arm chair with herringbone seat and back pattern. Photo courtesy of Shaker Workshops, *www.shakerworkshops.com*.

Scott Woody of Woody's Chair Shop created this traditional footstool frame. Diamond variation woven by Dave Klingler of *www.gochairrepair.com*, Asheville, NC. Photo by Tipton Gentry of Portable Onsite Photography. Courtesy of Planet Art/Chair Repair, *www.gochairrepair.com*.

Scott Woody of Woody's Chair Shop made this non-traditional frame, which is finished with a colorful seat woven by Dave Klingler of *www.gochairrepair.com*, Asheville, NC. Photo by Tipton Gentry of Portable Onsite Photography. Courtesy of Planet Art/Chair Repair, *www.gochairrepair.com*.

"Old Blue" salvaged chair with a Native American-inspired pattern designed and woven by Dave Klingler of *www.gochairrepair.com*, Asheville, NC. Photo by Tipton Gentry of Portable Onsite Photography. Courtesy of Planet Art/Chair Repair, *www.gochairrepair.com*.

CHAPTER 3

Rush Seats

Traditionally, rush for chair seats was made of twisted cattail leaves. Today, it is more common to use a tough-grade, fiber paper twisted into long strands, known as "fiber rush." It is sold by the pound and comes in three sizes: $\frac{4}{32}$ inch for fine work, $\frac{5}{32}$ inch for most chairs, and $\frac{6}{32}$ inch for larger pieces and patio furniture. Online suppliers are usually good sources of advice for the appropriate size and the amount of rush needed for a particular project. Before applying rush to a seat frame, make sure the glue used to assemble the chair has cured completely. The rush will exert a moderate amount of tension on the joints when it is installed.

Rushing a chair seat is simpler than caning because it involves repeating a single technique all around the seat frame. While chairs of any shape can be given a rush seat, it is best to learn the rushing technique on chairs with square seats and with front legs that extend slightly above the seat rails. This additional height will support the weave as it is wrapped around the corners. Seats that are not square need a few preliminary weaves across the side and front rails to create parallel sides, as shown on page 27, before rushing can begin.

Before starting, wrap the rush in loops around you hand to your elbow and dunk it in water for about 2 seconds, then shake the excess water from the rush. Always pull the rush tightly around the rails and keep adjacent rows as close together as possible.

RUSH SEAT

Early Shaker chairs, like the Enfield chair showm here, were finished with rush seats. Traditionally, the rush was natural, consisting of marsh grass twisted into a cord which was woven in a center diamond pattern over the frame. Rush seats are both comfortable and durable, and can be done in 4–5 hours or so once you get the knack.

This section shows how to rush a chair seat with a more contemporary material—tough-grade, fiber paper twisted into long strands, known as fiber or manila rush.

A fiber rush seat is woven onto a Shaker-inspired Enfield chair. Using this traditional material and the simple technique for installing it can impart a charming appearance to any stick-style chair.

A simple rush seat can give a charming old chair, like the one shown here, a new lease on life.

RUSHING A CHAIR SEAT

Bridging the front rail

If the seat rails do not form a square, you will need to use rush to create a square frame. Measure the difference in length between the longer and shorter rails—in this case, the front and back rails—and divide your measurement in half. Measure your result along the front rail from each of the front legs and make a mark on the rail. Cut a length of dampened rushing from a coil that is about twice the length of the front rail and tack it to the inside of a side rail about 2 inches from the front leg. Use an awl to create a hole in the side rail for the tack, then use the tack to punch a hole through the rush and attach it to the chair. Now loop the rush around the front rail from underneath, then around the side rail from underneath. Bring the rush across the front rail and loop it around the other side rail and the front rail in the same manner *(right)*. Holding the rush taut, tack it to the side rail opposite the first tack.

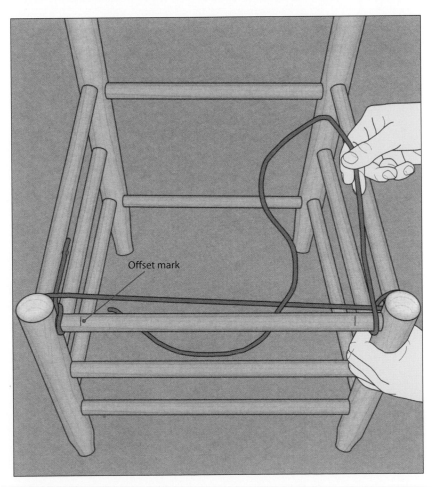

Offset mark

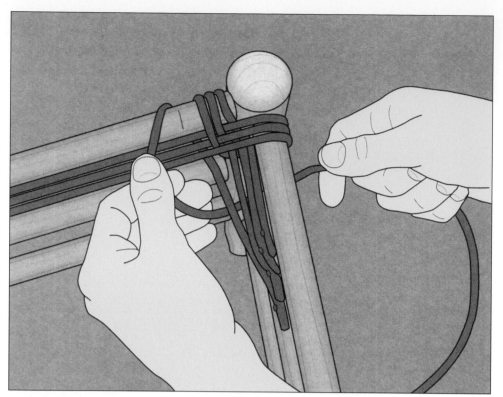

Squaring the seat frame
Fasten a length of rush alongside the first one, using the technique described on page 26. Loop it around the front and side rails and fasten it to the opposite rail. Continue adding lengths of rush *(left)* until you reach the offset marks you made on the front rail. To keep the rush as tight and straight as possible, tack the end, loop it as described, and then clamp the other end to the side rail to keep the tension as you tack the rush in place.

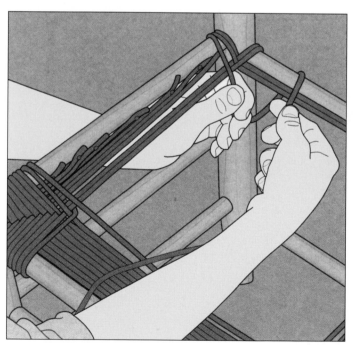

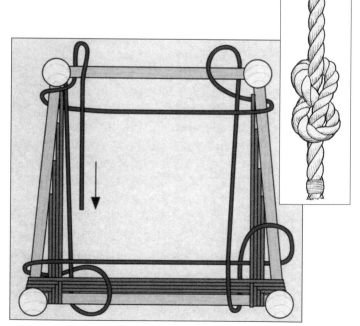

Weaving a complete circuit
Once you have squared the seat frame, you can begin rushing the seat all around the frame. Working with an approximately 20-foot length of rush, tack it to the side rail near the rear legs and loop it around all the rails *(above, left)*. Each complete circuit is known as a bout. Keep working around the chair using the same pattern *(above, right)*, clamping the rush every four bouts

or so to maintain the tension. Every six or seven bouts, use a screwdriver to tap the rush toward the corners of the chair to keep the weave even. When you get to the end of a length of rush, clamp it temporarily to the seat frame to keep it taut and attach it to a new piece using a figure-eight knot *(inset)*. Locate the knots on the underside of the seat so that they will not be visible.

Checking the weave for square

Once every third or fourth circuit, check whether the sides of the seat are perpendicular to each other. Holding the length of rush in a coil with one hand, butt a try square in one corner of the seat (*right*). The handle and blade of the square should rest flush against the rushing. If not, use a flat-tip screwdriver to straighten the side that is out-of-square, pushing the last circuit you installed against adjacent ones. Repeat at the remaining corners of the seat.

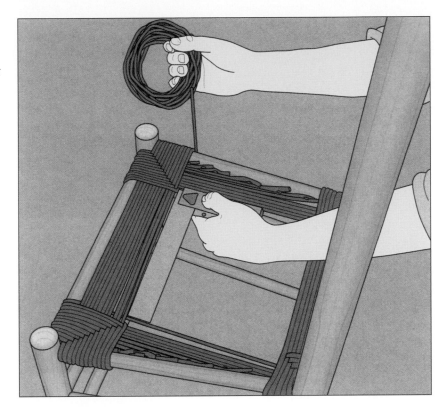

Stuffing the seat

Once the rushing is about two-thirds done, it is time to stuff the seat. (The stuffing provides extra padding). To prevent the rush from slackening, use a spring clamp to secure the loose length you are installing to a seat rail. Use cardboard for the padding, cutting one triangular piece for each side of the seat so that each triangle's long side is slightly shorter than the seat rail. Slip the padding under the rushing (*left*), then trim the tips if they overlap in the center. Continue the normal circuit as before until the two side rails are covered.

Spring clamp

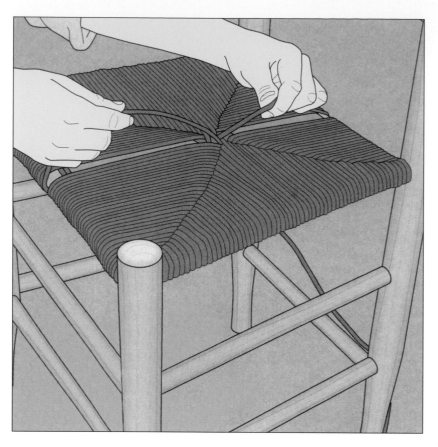

Completing the bridge

On a seat that is deeper than it is wide, as in the chair shown here, the rushing being installed on the side rails will meet in the middle of the seat before the rush on the front and back rails. Once this occurs, use a technique known as bridging to fill the gap. Loop the rushing on the front and back rails with a figure-eight pattern weave, passing the rush over the back rail, down through the center, under the seat, and up around the front rail. Then bring the rush over the seat from the front rail and back down through the center *(left)*. Pass the rush under the seat, come up around the back rail again, and repeat.

Finishing the job

Once you have bridged the gap between the front and back rails, set the chair upside down on a work table and tack the last strand of rush to the underside of the back seat rail *(right)*, or knot the rush in place in the center of the seat. If desired, coat the rush with a clear coat of shellac. Recoat the rush with shellac every 5–10 years to keep your chair seat looking like new.

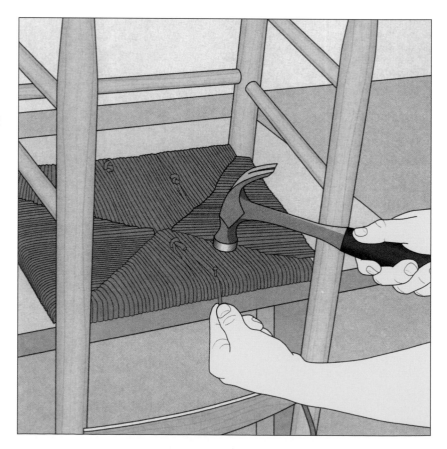

Index

More Great Books from Fox Chapel Publishing

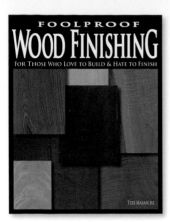

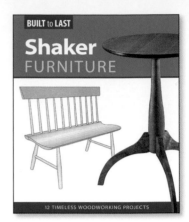
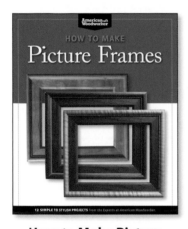